Sunshine

Jaclyn Spiezia

BookLeaf
Publishing

India | USA | UK

Presentation by *BookLeaf Publishing*

Web: www.bookleafpub.com

E-mail: info@bookleafpub.com

ISBN: 9789360944322

First edition 2024

I dedicate this book to my mom, who continues to encourage me to write, and who calls me her "Sunshine". I hope this book brightens your day.

ACKNOWLEDGEMENT

I want to thank my mom, my dad, my sister, my brother and all my family, friends, and teachers who have always supported me.

PREFACE

May we all have the courage to share our light,
even when skies are gray.

Sunshine

When I was little you called me Sunshine
And you held my hand through stormy rains.
You promised me that there was light inside me
And you showed me how to cast my rays.
Because if you, I felt bright
Even on days when I failed to see my light.
Because of you, I was happy
Even when things did not go my way.
Through my pain, my losses and my hardest
days
You were always there, reassuring me that I'd be
okay.
Still you say that I'm your sunshine,
But for me me, mom, you have always been
mine.

Books

I learned to love books
Not because of the stories within them
Or how the words were organized on the pages.
I learned to love books
Because I saw you sitting and reading.
There is as always one in your hand
So I knew that books were important,
That smart women read books
And you shared them with me.
You read to me every night
But it was your reading to me that was so special
I wanted to be like you
And so before I knew how to read
Or what the words on the pages meant,
I held books in my hands.
I learned to read books
Because you made me excited to learn how to
Dear Mom,
I learned to love books
Because I love you

Milk Time

Every morning started with a hug
And every night ended with milk and cookies
Many days I wish I could return
To when I was young and life felt so easy
To watching Scooby Doo re-runs
To playing at the Noodle Park
To swimming in the pool
To small hill sleigh rides
To dancing in the kitchen to a Beatles song
To the way things were before
Back when I was young

Journey through Time

Time has swallowed up the moments
That I've wanted to keep
Some nights I drink hot chocolate
And stay up late watching TV
The minutes continue to pass
Until I doze off on the couch
But no one ever told me
That the clock was ticking faster
As I grew up and moved out
How many years has it been
Since I first left home?
I recently did the math
And realized it was a decade ago
It has been 10 years since I first left
Now with 2 degrees, and jobs (past)
I recognize time went by fast
But my journey is not nearly finished yet
Still I often think about
When it will be time again
To return back to where I began
Before my time runs out

Lettuce

A brave little birdy once told me to eat some lettuce. I asked him why he'd said it. He told me it was the color of happiness and earth. If I had ingested it, I'd know my worth. I tried to bite into it, but every time I got close, my throat would stiffen, and I'd crinkle my nose. I'd expected it to taste badly. I'd thought all good things did, comparing it to when I had to drink cough medicine. Finally, I took a bite. I'd been tired of waiting. Now there was not turning back, but I'd expected it to change things. I thought I'd immediately feel that energy, but I didn't. And so I decided to eat all the green that I could see. I ate and I ate, until it hurt, but no matter the color, my mood didn't turn 8' fast, I was sadder, and even more uncertain, of what I should be doing. I'd been sitting in my room in the darkness, and I decided to open up my curtains. Outside the sky was grey, and the water was blue, the tree bark was brown, and then suddenly I knew. It's not about eating lettuce. It's about trying. Jumping off a branch, is the only way to begin flying.

Amphibian

Some wonder how great it could be
To be able to live
Spend your time
Where you please
On land
In the water
It must be cool, they all say
But being in two places
And never really belonging in either
It's not fun
You don't understand why
They all want to be like you
Because they wouldn't if any of them
Had an idea at all
What it is like to be left out
Where you should fit in

Illusive Sea Glass

She runs, far away from everyone
But she isn't that far away
You can see her on the horizon
But when you offer her clay
There comes from her lips no response
She is far away
 Far away in her thoughts.

The pressure, it built up into glass
When she neglects to hear you,
You become quite crass.
Her ears are listening to
The sounds from the depths of the deep royal
blue.
In her mind she is swimming beneath
All of the stress that is above reach.
She is lost in a calm piece of sea glass that she is
inside
Why she's not yet answered you, you can't
believe
But the glass is invisible to the human eye.
You don't see how she's dealing with her pain
Or how her peaceful swim becomes one of
strain.

If you knew the strength of the stressful currents
you would have urged her to keep her head
 Above water.
Because trapped underneath with no way to
breathe and no one to help her because she is
inside a wall of sea glass that can't be broken,
that's invisible, and because she had hardly ever
spoken about these issues, you can't resolve.
Now you can't see her at all.
You run forth because she's disappeared
But because all you could feel was ignorance
You have no way to know that
The ocean floor found her, dead.
You walk away upset.
Then blame everyone else when her body
washes up on shore
But slowly sea glass builds around yourself.
And you realize what you didn't before.

Clipping

The ground felt warm under my toes
Few slicked grass smelt like freedom
Growth; crisp air cuddled my nose
Auburn hues littered clean a forest kingdom.

Shifting lights; hazed reflection
Foam and salt mixed together
Scattered sounds, yet vacancies in all directions.
Fighting climb and falling surrender

Brittles flowers strung from vines
Nervous smiles, and reasonless anxieties
Laughter, spontaneity, disaster lines
Crowded spaces in between societies.

Heavy thoughts seem lighter
Pie feed my hungry desire
Wearing jeans that had once fit tighter
Teal is now hung from the wire.

Coming up for air
Clipping strings once taut
Restyling my hair
Better than I thought

Tortoise

I am a tortoise
Not because I have a shell
But because I move slowly
It takes time for me to
Get places not because I am slow
But because I tend to travel fast
If I do not monitor my movements
Purposefully.

I am a tortoise
Yet I only truly use my shell
For protection from the people I care most for.

Pocket of Peace

The first words are always the hardest
There is a calmness in the silence
Complacent in stillness, yet never complicit.
Take a dee breath and let it all sink in.
The warm water feels comforting on my skin.
If it's deep enough, shall I just dive in?
Currently I am floating
Moving with the liquid that is sudsy and
foaming.
Afraid to look beneath to see how deep.
Wouldn't want to disrupt this pocket of peace.
If I swam to leave, I'm unsure I could turn back
Right now I am one with the spring on my back.
Departure is only desired by a return
Ruining my comfort and the peace, I weigh the
worth
Just as I am about to move
A bite on my toe takes me by surprise
And I scream into the silence
Breaking the serenity with my cry.

The Best is Yet to Come

The best is yet to come
And has already been
For as long as souls have cycled the earth
Goodness has been like sin
Hear the swallow mourn the dawn
As the moon sinks into the skies
The gravity that bears earth's weight is ever a
surprise
Hold right the covers as you hide underneath
The mistakes you have made reset in your sleep.
Destined to end; yearning for time; repeating
again
Synchronized by rhyme;
First came the chicken
Crack open the egg, scramble your insides
Pin your peg, wed your brides
The sun always sets before it can rise

Sky Ship

I fear my heart as it races ahead of my brain.
The blood pumps so fast, there isn't time to
breathe
Oxygen is lost, and it becomes hard to think.
Butterflies is a term that could pass to describe it
because it feels like I'm flying above in a sky
ship.
Crash,
I've separated from the rocket
Now I'm floating into orbit
I can't feel my extremities
My vibes are getting weak
Space is cold
And it is scary
But I'm still breathing air in
From my oxygen tank
And I'll keep going
I was panicking
Thinking I had none left
I worked my mind into a mess
But as I gaze out to the mass
That is the moon
I don't feel lost or scared
Life is beautiful when viewed out here.
And even though I'm uncertain where
I am, I know soon enough
I will land

Wingless

On the playground the children found
A little ladybug
They asked what was wrong
Why was it not flying above anymore?
A teacher went over and lifted it up
Exclaiming it had broke wings
One of the children asked,
"Can I poke it with this stick thing?"

The teacher said, "Of course not" and tried to
rescue it to safety, placing it on a tree leaf where
it could be happy.
Only a few moments later something dropped on
my shoulder, I squirmed about to flick it, and
realized
the little bug had fallen back over

I thought about my own wings,
the ones I never used to fly
And I realized that I fly now more
Even though I abstain from getting high
Without wings
And without the funneled wind
A little bit of luck comes from within

I don't have my wings
But I will be okay.
A little bit of luck, goes a long way.

Little Soldiers

Butter bröt
Nicht mit crust
Perfect squares
Grandpa chopped up

One by one
In my grip
Little soldiers
Are no match
For my lips

Acorn

You are not a lost cause
Just because you went a season without being
planted, does not mean you are useless

Just because time passed and the other oaks
grew taller, doesn't mean you have less of a
capacity

Because you see,
With time we all grow
And some seeds are still waiting to be planted,
traveling through the leaves and snow.
But you've survived the squirrels, and the
storms.
I have hope for you, I really do.
Grow strong and steady, acorn.

Woman, I

Women inspire
Women inquire
Innocent women can still ignite fires

Never ignore a woman's desires

Women resist
Women persist
Intelligent women have iron fists

Never underestimate a woman's grit

Women endure
Women explore
Irresistible women wear invincible armor

Never challenge a woman's decor

Women imagine
Women envision
Incredible women are investigating missions

Never forget a woman's existence

Am a woman, I
A woman, I am
I am a woman

Never stopped by any man

The Lifecycle of a Bubble

I begged the floor to release me from its gravity
I floated upwards towards eternity
I flew out the window and up to the sky
But all at once, I was getting too high
I floated past squirrels seated on branches
I swirled between birds in heated matches
I drifted over pastures
And looked down at rivers
I might just be a bubble
But I began to shiver
The higher I went
The colder it got
And then
I heard
Myself
Go
POP!

Time Plate

The plate held my time
It was served for me to eat
Not a bite was had

I thought I should wait
Because it was so precious
Not to be had fast

Only one per person
Or so that's what I was told
Waiting was easy

But soon I grew old
And my time was running out
Yet still I waited

The perfect moment
To indulge from my platter
When would it arrive?

Soon I was to die
And so I picked up my plate
Ready to dig in

But to my surprise

There was nothing left on it
My plate was empty

Where had the time gone?
I had waited patiently
Not a bite was had

I waited too long
To enjoy the gift given
And now it was gone

Just like my life was
Though I waited long; it went fast
Suddenly it passed

And I had missed out
On the life I could have had
Because I waited

Waiting can be good
And maybe necessary
But not all the time

Before you know it
Time will have passed too quickly
Right before your eyes